FROM POLE TO POLE

The graceful and elegant Arctic tern flies from the top of the world to the bottom and back again every year – a round trip of some 40,000 km (25,000 miles). It flies farther than any other bird to spend summer in both the Arctic and the Antarctic. The Arctic tern probably experiences more hours of daylight than any other creature on Earth.

ICY PENGUINS

These penguins are resting on a rare blue iceberg. About seven species of penguin live and breed in south polar regions.

CHANGING CLIMATES

The poles have not always been so cold. Ice has built up at the poles only during the last 30 million years and the lands around the Arctic and under the Antarctic ice have been in their current positions for less than 50 million years. The continent of Antarctica was probably once near the Equator where the climate was warmer and subtropical. Ferns, cycads, trees and other green plants grew there and dinosaurs roamed the land. We know little about the prehistoric origins of the Arctic region but the landmasses have drifted slowly about and sea levels have changed. This has sometimes allowed land bridges to form between continents such as Asia and North America, along which animals could migrate.

Dawn redwood fossils dating back 100 million years have been found in the Arctic.

Fierce dinosaurs, such as Allosaurus, once lived in the Antarctic.

NORTH

THE POLES TODAY

The geographic poles are at the extreme ends of the globe at the points farthest north and farthest south in the world. A magnetic pole lies near each of the geographic poles, but they are always moving. Compasses work using a magnetic needle so they point to magnetic north and south rather than the true poles.

SOUTH

WEATHER & CLIMATE

SNOW BLIZZARDS

Strong winds draw heat away from the body and make animals very cold. Sitting curled up with its back to the wind, this husky is trying to expose as little as possible of its body to the freezing wind. Its thick fur helps to keep it warm.

Polar climates are intensely cold and dry, with very strong winds. Cold air moves from the poles towards the Equator, helping to stop the Earth from getting too hot. Antarctica is the coldest and windiest place on Earth, with average winter temperatures of -60°C (-76°F) and roaring, ferocious winds of up to 300 km/h (180 mph) producing blizzards and snow drifts. An unprotected person could freeze solid in minutes. Both the Arctic and the Antarctic are cold deserts, since most areas receive less than 240 mm (10 inches) of rain or snow each year. Yet more than nine-tenths of all the world's fresh water is stored in the ice sheets on Antarctica and Greenland. Polar regions have only two seasons, summer and winter. When it is summer in the Arctic, it is winter in the Antarctic, and vice versa. The 24 hours of daylight in summer have led to the nickname 'lands of the midnight Sun', because the Sun is still shining in the sky at midnight.

POLE to POLE

(3)

R

POLE TO POLE

Wild, icy cold and spectacularly beautiful, the polar regions extend for over 2,000 km (1,200 miles) in all directions around the North Pole and the South Pole. They are the last two wilderness areas on Earth. A vast area of frozen ocean, the Arctic Ocean, surrounds the North Pole, while the South Pole is surrounded by a frozen continent called Antarctica. Antarctica is the fifth largest continent and has 90 per cent of all the ice on Earth. Both the Arctic and the Antarctic have long, dark winters when the Sun never shines. During the short, cool summers, the Sun never sets and many animals visit polar lands to feed, nest and raise their young. Only a few especially hardy animals manage to live in the Arctic and Antarctic all year round.

ARCTIC TRAVEL

The harsh terrain and the savage and unpredictable climate combine to make polar travel dangerous and exhausting. In the Arctic, native peoples originally used long, low sleds pulled by husky dogs – bred from Arctic wolves – to transport heavy loads. Huskies are hardy, strong and intelligent and work in a strict hierarchy under the lead dog. It usually takes a year or two to learn how to drive a dog sled. Dog sleds are still one of the best ways to travel in polar regions, but most polar transport is now motorized and includes vehicles such as snowmobiles or skidoos.

ARCTIC SUMMER

Caribou (also called reindeer) visit Arctic lands in summer when the top layer of the ground thaws and there are plenty of plants for them to eat. Unfortunately for them, clouds of midges, gnats and mosquitoes also swarm over the marshy ground in summer. The insects are, however, useful food for some of the birds that visit the Arctic for the summer season.

CURTAINS OF LIGHT

Glowing, shimmering curtains of light called auroras sometimes appear in polar skies, especially near the magnetic poles. They happen because the Earth's magnetic poles attract charged particles given off by the Sun. When these particles strike gas particles in the Earth's atmosphere, coloured light is radiated. Auroras are called the *Aurora Borealis,* or Northern Lights, in the Arctic and the *Aurora Australis,* or Southern Lights, in the Antarctic. Auroras are difficult to photograph because they are very faint and move rapidly.

WHY ARE THE POLES COLD?

The Sun's rays bring heat and light to the Earth. But the Earth is curved like a ball, so the Sun's rays are weaker and more spread out at the poles than at the Equator. The rays also have to travel farther through the atmosphere to reach the poles and the atmosphere absorbs much of the heat, making the poles colder. The white ice and snow at the poles reflect back between 50 and 90 per cent of the Sun's heat, making the poles colder still.

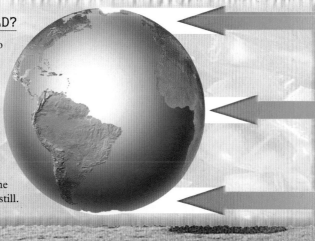

THE NORTH POLE

Although the areas around the North Pole and the South Pole are both cold places and home to many similar animals, they have a very different geography. The North Pole lies in the middle of a shallow, frozen ocean surrounded by the northern edges of Europe, Asia and North America. This whole area is called the Arctic, named after Arktos, the Great Bear star constellation, which dominates the northern polar skies.

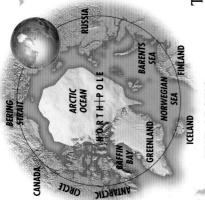

THE ARCTIC

The Arctic region consists mainly of the Arctic Ocean, which can be as much as 1,600 km (1,000 miles) across and has a thin skin of ice on top. The largest island in the Arctic Ocean is Greenland, which is covered in a thick ice sheet. Also part of the Arctic is a band of land called the tundra, which means 'treeless land'. This covers the northern parts of Canada, Alaska, Russia and Scandinavia. On maps, an imaginary line called the Arctic Circle surrounds the Arctic area.

LIVING IN THE ARCTIC

Polar bears are the only animals to live and hunt on top of the Arctic Ocean – polar bear tracks have even been found near the North Pole itself. There are probably about 20,000 polar bears wandering alone over the remote Arctic ice floes as they hunt for seals beneath the ice.

THE ARCTIC ICE

In winter, the ice covers an area 1½ times the size of Canada, but the edges melt in summer.

The sea bed is a pitch-dark world of underwater mountains, ranges of hills and vast, flat plains.

The middle of the Arctic is frozen all year round, although the ice is less than 10 metres (33 ft) thick.

ASIA

NORTH AMERICA

ARCTIC FLOWERS

The tundra landscape is low and flat, with no trees, but many low bushes, lichens, mosses and grasses.

In summer, parts of the tundra burst into bloom as flowering plants rush to flower and produce seeds before the short spell of warm weather ends. There are over 500 species of flowering plants in the Arctic.

BERING STRAIT

RUSSIA

BARENTS SEA

FINLAND

ARCTIC OCEAN

NORTH POLE

NORWEGIAN SEA

ICELAND

GREENLAND

BAFFIN BAY

CANADA

ANTARCTIC CIRCLE

THE SOUTH POLE

The South Pole lies in the middle of the continent of Antarctica – the name means 'opposite the Arctic'. Antarctica is a mountainous continent that is almost completely covered by a gigantic ice sheet and is the size of Europe and the USA put together. Unlike the Arctic, the Antarctic has very little ice-free land, even in summer. It has no land mammals, and fewer plants and animals than the Arctic.

THE ANTARCTIC

The Antarctic region is separated from the rest of the world by the stormy waters of the Southern Ocean. In winter, ice extends hundreds of kilometres out into the ocean from Antarctic coasts. There are several groups of remote islands near Antarctica (such as South Georgia), but the nearest landmass is the southern tip of South America, which is about 960 km (600 miles) away. On maps, the Antarctic region is bordered by an imaginary line called the Antarctic Circle.

ANTARCTIC ICE

More than half of the surface of Antarctica lies below sea level.

A few mountains, called nunataks, extend their peaks above the ice.

If the ice was removed, the land would rise about 550 metres (1,800 ft).

The Antarctic continent is almost completely covered by a gigantic ice sheet, up to 4 km (2.5 miles) thick.

WEST   EAST

WINTER IN ANTARCTICA

Penguins live only in the southern half of the world, mainly in and around Antarctica, so polar bears and penguins never meet. Only two species of penguin, the Adélie and the emperor, breed on the Antarctic continent itself. Most penguins leap ashore to breed during the summer, but the emperor penguin (as seen here) lays its eggs in the winter. This allows the chicks to hatch in early spring and have the whole summer to grow.

ANTARCTIC FLOWERS

Only two flowering plants grow on Antarctica and neither of them looks much like a flowering plant because they have tiny, drab-coloured flowers. The most common is Antarctic hairgrass (above) and the other is a type of pearlwort called *Colobanthus*.

POLAR PLANTS

It is amazing that any plants survive at all in polar lands because of the short summers, thin soils, searing cold winds and lack of moisture. In the Arctic, the soil is permanently frozen below the surface but the top layer thaws in summer. Water cannot drain away, so the waterlogged summer soil is boggy and marshy with many lakes and ponds. Arctic plants have to cope with these wet soils as well as the cold and dry air. They tend to grow close to the ground in tussocks, cushions, carpets and rosettes to keep out of the wind, to trap moisture and to avoid being crushed by snow and ice. The leaves of polar plants are often thick and waxy with few breathing holes to stop water escaping.

MEAT-EATING PLANTS

Sundews gain extra nutrients by trapping insects on their sticky flypaper leaves. The leaves are covered with special hairs that have drops of sticky glue on the ends. Any insect attracted to the glistening drops is likely to become trapped on the sticky hairs. The leaf then slowly curls around the insect's body and the hairs pour out digestive juices to turn the body into a soupy pulp. The plant absorbs its insect soup and, after a day or so, all that is left of the insect is a dry, empty husk.

ANCIENT LICHENS

In both polar regions, the most successful plants are mosses, lichens and algae. There are over 400 different lichens in the Antarctic, some of which are at least 10,000 years old but still very small because they grow extremely slowly in the cold conditions.

ARCTIC WILLOW IN AUTUMN

Although there are no tall trees on the tundra, the remarkable Arctic willow manages to survive by creeping along the ground. Its branches never rise more than 10 cm (4 inches) from the ground, but may be more than 5 m (16ft) long. Its shoots and leaves contain more vitamin C than an orange.

ARCTIC POPPY

The bowl-shaped flowers of the Arctic poppy work like a reflecting dish to focus the Sun's rays onto the central part of the flower. The flower also turns to follow the path of the Sun. Both these adaptations help to keep the seeds warm so they will develop quickly – before the summer Sun disappears from the sky. Arctic poppies grow in low cushions, like many polar plants.

POLLINATION

The hairy 'fur' on a bumblebee helps it to keep warm but few insects can survive in these cold places. Most Arctic plants cannot rely on insects to carry their pollen. Instead it is spread by strong winds from plant to plant so that seeds can grow. Many plants reproduce by growing new pieces of themselves, such as small bulbs or creeping stems called runners.

TUNDRA PLANTS

On the Arctic tundra in the short northern summer, there are colourful, flower-filled meadows. Some of the flowers produce their seeds inside berries, such as bilberries, cranberries, bunch berries, raspberries and crowberries. Many Arctic plants such as bilberries are self-pollinating, which means they use their own pollen to produce seeds. This means that they do not have to rely on the wind, or insects, to spread the pollen. The new plants, which grow from the seeds, are identical to their parent plants.

FROM FLOWER TO SEED

Since the Arctic summer is so short, plants such as this purple saxifrage must produce their seeds and ripen them in one season. The seeds must be ready to sprout or germinate as soon as possible the following summer. They spend the winter resting in the soil, waiting for the warmth and moisture they need to trigger germination.

PLANT EATERS

The leaves, shoots, roots and berries of tundra plants provide food for a variety of animals, including this brown bear. Bears eat as much as possible in the summer to build up stores of fat which will last them through the winter. There is even a berry called a bearberry.

ARCTIC ANIMALS

From tiny, buzzing insects and scurrying lemmings to huge caribou, polar bears, whales and walruses, the Arctic and tundra lands are full of a surprising variety of animals, both in the sea and on the land. Many mammals and birds are migrants, moving north in summer from the lands or seas outside the Arctic Circle. These include caribou (reindeer), ducks, geese, swans, wading birds and some seals, which visit the Arctic to feed and breed. This means that the number and variety of Arctic animals change dramatically with the seasons. The few hardy Arctic residents include musk oxen, polar bears, some seals and whales, Arctic foxes, and birds such as the ptarmigan and ivory gull. Unlike the Antarctic, there are land birds as well as sea birds. Summer lakes and bogs provide breeding grounds for millions of mosquitoes and other biting flies, while flowering plants on the tundra attract butterflies, bees and beetles.

SEALS

The most numerous and widespread seal resident in the Arctic is the ringed seal, which may even appear at the North Pole. The other main Arctic seals, the harp seal (above) and the hooded seal, are migrants. Some harp seals travel about 3,500 km (2,000 miles) to give birth on Arctic ice floes in late winter. By the time the seal pups are old enough to hunt on their own, summer has arrived and there are plenty of fish in the sea.

THE ARCTIC FRITILLARY BUTTERFLY

The Arctic fritillary is one of the few butterflies found within the Arctic Circle and is one of only about six species of butterfly to survive in Greenland. Its dark markings help to absorb warmth from the Sun and the speckled pattern on its wings camouflage it from enemies, such as birds and spiders.

WALRUSES

Living only in the Arctic, walruses are not seals, but are closely related to them.
Both male and female walruses have two long, sharp, curved tusks, which are actually upper canine teeth. In fights, walruses attack each other with their tusks. Walruses use their fleshy noses and whiskers to find clams and other shellfish, crabs and worms on the sea bed.

LEMMINGS

Tunnelling among Arctic plants, rocks or soils are large numbers of lemmings. These small rodents are plant-eaters, which form an important source of food for meat-eating animals, such as Arctic foxes, stoats and owls. Lemmings make ball-shaped nests out of plant material and females often give birth to the first litter of the year beneath the snow at the end of winter. If there is plenty of food, one female can have as many as 84 young in one year.

THE LITTLE AUK

There are no penguins in the Arctic but little auks, or dovekies, look rather like them. They have come to look similar because they have adapted to a similar environment. Both birds have a streamlined shape for swimming underwater and flipper-like wings. The main difference is that the little auk can fly, but penguins cannot. The little auk is not much bigger than a thrush but it is very successful at living in the Arctic.

WILD WOLVES

Although wolves live in a variety of habitats, they are well adapted to life in the Arctic. Their thick fur keeps them warm and often turns white for camouflage. This helps them to get close to their prey without being seen. Arctic wolves hunt in packs so they are able to catch large animals such as caribou and young musk oxen. They will also eat carrion and small mammals, such as voles, lemmings and hares. Superb hearing and a keen sense of smell allow a pack of wolves to track down its prey. The wolves relentlessly pursue their quarry for long distances without tiring thanks to their strong bodies and long legs.

LIFE IN SLOW MOTION

The cold temperature of the water and the scarcity of available food mean that life runs in slow motion and animals without backbones tend to grow slowly. They live longer and reach larger sizes than species from warmer places.

The sea bed around Antarctica is sometimes covered with countless red starfish, some of which can live for nearly 40 years.

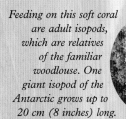

Sea spiders walk or crawl about on the ocean floor on their 10 or 12 long legs. They either suck the juices from soft-bodied animals or browse on hydroids and moss animals.

Feeding on this soft coral are adult isopods, which are relatives of the familiar woodlouse. One giant isopod of the Antarctic grows up to 20 cm (8 inches) long.

ANTARCTIC ANIMALS

There are few ice-free areas of land on the continent of Antarctica and the largest animal that lives on land all year round is a tiny wingless midge only 12 mm (0.5 inches) long. During the summer, however, the ice around the fringes of the continent melts and animals, such as penguins, seals and sea birds, come ashore to breed. On the islands around the Antarctic continent, the climate is less harsh and the greater variety of plant life encourages a greater variety of animal life, particularly birds such as albatrosses and petrels. Sheathbills are the only land birds to live all year round in Antarctica; other birds leave in the winter. Although life on the land is restricted by the ice and the climate, life in the seas around Antarctica is incredibly rich – twice as rich as in the Arctic. Small animals include plankton, corals, anemones, sponges, worms and starfish, and there are also larger creatures such as fish, seals and whales.

BLUE WHALE

The Southern Ocean around Antarctica has a greater variety and quantity of whales than any other ocean. They range from toothed whales, such as killer whales, to baleen whales, such as this blue whale. Baleen whales filter food through fringes of tough skin (called baleen) that hang down inside their mouths. Blue whales are the largest animals that have ever lived. Adults weigh more than 30 elephants and are longer than a jumbo jet.

BLUE-EYED SHAGS

The feathers of the blue-eyed shag soak up water so its weight increases and it can sink and dive after fish in the ocean. But after a swim, the bird has to spread out its wings to dry. Shags never fish far from their nest or roost sites and they use their rockeries all year round. Their rockeries are on remote Antarctic islands and the very northern tip of the Antarctic peninsula.

MINIBEASTS

The dominant land animals in Antarctica are tiny minibeasts called mites and springtails (right). Mites are related to spiders while springtails are wingless insects. Both have antifreeze in their bodies to stop them freezing to death. They reproduce whenever the temperature rises above freezing.

WEDDELL SEAL

Weddell seals spend the whole winter under the ice that covers the seas around Antarctica. They make breathing holes in the ice with their teeth and may have to grind through ice many metres thick. If they fail to keep their breathing holes open, the seals will drown. These hardy seals can dive to depths of about 580 m (1,900 ft) and stay underwater for up to 70 minutes. They communicate using a series of weird calls that bounce off the ice and carry for many kilometres underwater.

ADÉLIE PENGUINS

Adélie penguins spend the winter out at sea. When they return to their breeding colonies on the Antarctic continent in October, there is still a lot of sea ice between them and their nest sites. They have no time to wait for the ice to melt, so they march inland over the ice for distances of up to 100 km (62 miles).

Surviving the Cold

Animals living in both polar regions have similar adaptations to help them survive in these hostile environments. Thick layers of fur, feathers or fatty blubber help to keep out the cold and trap the heat given off by the body of a bird or a mammal. Many are forced to migrate to warmer places in the winter but a few small mammals (such as the Arctic ground squirrel) hibernate over the winter. Ice fish and some minibeasts survive all year round thanks to the antifreeze in their blood. The dark colours of minibeasts absorb the Sun's heat and help them to keep warm.

BLUBBER

The thick blubber of this baby seal stops body heat escaping. Blubber is a thick layer of fat under the skin. It can be up to 25 cm (10 inches) thick. Whales also rely on their blubber for warmth.

Cubs stay with their mother for a year or more to learn how to survive and hunt on their own.

Hairs in the coat are hollow and trap warm air near the body, like double glazing.

Under the fur, a thick layer of blubber insulates the bear against the cold and acts as a food store when food is hard to find.

Polar bear hairs are transparent, allowing the Sun's heat to penetrate through the fur to the skin, which is black and absorbs the heat.

BODY WARMTH

When emperor penguin chicks are about eight weeks old, they are too big to hide under their parents for warmth. Instead they huddle together and rely on their dense, fluffy feathers and the warm bodies of their fellow chicks to keep warm. Conditions are so hard in the Antarctic that only 19 per cent of emperor penguin chicks will survive their first year.

ANTIFREEZE

The antifreeze in the blood of ice fish stops ice crystals forming. In the middle of winter, when the top of the ocean is solid ice, these fish manage to survive in the almost frozen waters below. Fish without this adaptation would freeze to death in these conditions.

SHELTER

Wandering albatross chicks sit on the nest for up to a year through winter blizzards and snowstorms. They are protected from the cold by thick down feathers and an insulating layer of fat under the skin. The chick's survival depends on how successful its parents are at finding food in the stormy Southern Ocean.

Small round ears lose little heat.

POLAR BEARS

The polar bear of the Arctic is the largest bear in the world – an adult male can be nearly twice as tall as a person and six times as heavy. Its bulk helps it to keep warm, as does its thick fur coat which is made up of two layers, a thick underfur of short hairs, and an outer coat of long guard hairs. These hairs stick together when they get wet, forming a waterproof barrier.

A polar bear's nose is just about the only part of the body that is not furry.

Its big paws have rough, furry, non-slip soles to grip slippery snow and ice.

Yellow-white fur is useful for camouflage. The colour of the fur comes from the way the light reflects off the colourless, hollow hairs.

Powerful legs enable a polar bear to walk and swim long distances when hunting prey, although it becomes overheated after running for a long period of time.

ANIMALS ON THE MOVE

Walking and running over slippery ice and soft snow is not easy. Polar mammals and birds often have wide, flat feet with fur or feathers between the toes. This spreads out their weight like human snowshoes and stops them sinking into the snow. On slippery slopes, some penguins lie down on the snow and slide down like living toboggans. Polar birds that can fly need powerful wings to survive the strong winds and make long migration journeys. They need plenty of food to give them the energy to fly. Before migrating, they store energy in the form of fat in their bodies, as do the many polar animals who migrate to and from the Arctic and Antarctic every year. The blubber of whales, seals and penguins is a useful source of energy for their long journeys. It also helps to smooth out their body shape, making them more streamlined so they can swim faster and farther.

PORPOISING PENGUINS

In order to breathe while swimming fast, penguins often leap out of the water. They travel through the air at speeds of up to 25 km/h (16 mph). This technique of leaping in and out of the water is called porpoising. Under the water, penguins use their stiff wings to almost fly through the water. They steer with their feet and tails.

MIGRATION JOURNEYS

Caribou, or reindeer, are always on the move, trekking incredible distances of up to 9,000 km (5,600 miles) – the longest journeys of any land mammal on Earth. They move between forests on the edge of the Arctic, where they shelter in the winter, and the Arctic tundra, where they feed in summer. The caribou follow well-marked trails that are often hundreds of years old and usually cross many fast-flowing rivers. A line of migrating caribou may stretch for 300 km (190 miles).

JET SET

Torpedo-shaped squid are an ideal shape for shooting through the water fast. They use a method of jet propulsion to accelerate rapidly. By pushing a narrow jet of water out of a funnel at the front end of the body, the squid shoots off in the other direction, which is backwards. The funnel can be curved for swimming forwards. Larger squid can swim at up to 30 km/h (19 mph), very useful if they are escaping from predators such as sperm whales.

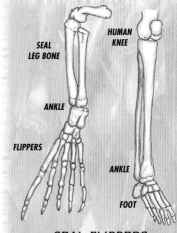

WIDE WINGS

The spectacular wandering albatross has the largest wingspan of any bird. It spends most of its life at sea gliding on its huge wings. The long, narrow shape of the wings is ideal for picking up the air currents and it glides at great speed for long distances, hardly beating its wings at all. It can reach speeds of 88 km/h (55 mph) and keep going for days at a time.

WHALE TAILS

The flat, rigid tail flukes of a whale move up and down to push it forwards through the water. Swimming movements are powered by large muscles lying above and below the backbone. About a third of a whale's body is pure muscle. The huge bulk of a whale's body is supported by the water pushing up against its skin. Its blubber also helps it to float more easily.

SEAL FLIPPERS

SEAL LEG BONE

HUMAN KNEE

ANKLE

FLIPPERS

ANKLE

FOOT

From the outside, the flipper of a seal looks very different from a human arm or foot. But inside, the bones are the same. As seals have evolved over millions of years, their limbs have become webbed paddles, which push them through the water faster than our hands and feet. The flipper has a bigger surface without gaps and pushes more water out of the way at each stroke. True seals use their back flippers for swimming; sea lions and fur seals use their front flippers instead.

SNOWSHOE FEET

Arctic hares have wide, flat feet with lots of fur underneath. This helps them to run or walk over snow without sinking in very far. Their long back legs allow them to bound along quickly, which is vitally important when they are escaping from predators such as Arctic foxes.

LAND FOOD CHAIN

ARCTIC FOX

↓

ARCTIC HARE

↓

LEAVES & BERRIES

Land food chains are very different in the Arctic and Antarctic. The Arctic has a lot of land plants for plant-eaters such as Arctic hares, which in turn are prey to meat-eaters like Arctic foxes. The Antarctic has very few plants. A typical food chain might be a plant-eating mite feeding on fungi and being eaten in turn by a meat-eating mite.

PACK POWER

Hunting in packs of up to 20 animals, gray wolves range over large areas to find enough food to eat. They can run for many hours, tiring out their prey. Many packs follow migrating herds of caribou, picking off old, young and sick animals that stray from the main herd.

The wolves disable their prey by biting its legs and hindquarters, then kill with a bite to the throat.

PREDATORS & PREY

In polar oceans, predators and their prey are remarkably similar in both the Arctic and the Antarctic. Killer whales are top predators in both polar regions. They attack in groups, like wolves on dry land, which allows them to catch and kill bigger animals than they could on their own. Predators are usually strong, fierce animals, with sharp teeth, claws or beaks to help them catch their prey. They often have to move very fast to catch up with their next meal before it escapes. Food is scarce in polar regions and predators may go without food for five days or more.

PATIENT HUNTER

To catch a ringed seal, a polar bear waits patiently for a seal to come up for air. Its white coat makes it blend into the white, snowy background as it keeps still and silent for up to four hours. As soon as the seal comes to the surface, the polar bear pounces, killing the seal with a blow from its huge paws and a bite at the back of the skull. The bear is so powerful, it can drag a seal out of the water through a small hole in the ice several metres thick.

SEA CATS

Like their spotted namesakes on land, leopard seals are strong, swift, solitary hunters. They hide in the water near penguin colonies, making surprise attacks on penguin chicks learning to swim. Chicks make easy prey because they are not very good at diving, so have little chance of escape. The leopard seal often plays with its victim for 10 minutes or more. Then it beats the dead penguin chicks against the surface of the water, stripping their feathers off and turning the skin inside out to get at the flesh. Leopard seals also eat other seals, squid, fish and krill.

FIERCE AND FURRY

The wolverine is strong for its size and has a powerful, crushing bite. Its large feet allow it to chase after its prey up to a distance of 65 km (40 miles) before it needs a rest. Once it has made a kill, a wolverine quickly takes the body of its victims to pieces, hiding most of the meat to eat later, when food may be hard to find.

SOUTHERN STINKERS

Giant petrels are nicknamed 'stinkers' after their unpleasant smell. They are about the size of a vulture and use their powerful hooked beaks to kill penguins, shags and squid, as well as to tear the meat from seal carcasses.

ARCTIC PREDATORS

There are more predatory birds in the Arctic than the Antarctic because of the variety of small mammals on tundra lands. Snowy owls, like this one, feed mainly on lemmings, swooping down to catch them in their strong, curved talons.

OCEAN FOOD CHAIN

KILLER WHALE

↓

SEAL

↓

SQUID

↓

KRILL

↓

PLANT PLANKTON

In polar waters, killer whales are top predators feeding on seals and penguins. Sea birds and squid prey on fish and tiny animals and plants, called plankton, that float in the water.

SLIPPERY MOUTHFUL

Puffins have special spines on the tongue and top part of the bill. These help them to catch and hold slippery fish, such as sand eels, and carry them back for their chicks. One puffin can hold up to 60 small fish at a time. Puffins catch their food by diving and chasing their fishy prey underwater.

DEFENCE

Penguins zooming through the water, caribou galloping across the tundra, snow geese flying up out of reach of Arctic foxes...one of the best means of defence is to move as fast as possible. There is also safety in numbers. Herds of mammals, flocks of birds and shoals of fish help each other to spot danger and may co-operate to drive predators away. Nesting in remote and inaccessible places, such as remote Antarctic islands or steep sea cliffs, also reduces the chances of being attacked. Some prey animals try to avoid being seen by having camouflaged fur or feathers that match their surroundings. But not all prey animals are cowards; some have formidable weapons, such as horns or tusks, and are prepared to stand and fight for their survival.

SEA BIRD COLONIES

By nesting in large colonies on steep, rocky cliffs, sea birds make it very difficult for predators to reach their chicks and eggs. Birds will dive-bomb predators that get too close and shriek alarm calls to their fellow nesters. Birds that nest in cliff-top burrows, such as puffins, are also well hidden from the eyes of their enemies.

HEAD TO HEAD

Although this polar bear has the advantage of sheer size, the walrus has its tusks to use as weapons against such predators. Its very thick, leathery skin is also useful against the polar bear's sharp teeth and claws. Walruses are fiercely protective of their young, which could be the reason for this stand-off.

COLOUR CHANGE

Many Arctic animals have different coats in different seasons. In winter, the ptarmigan is white so it is hard to see against a snowy landscape. In summer, when the snow has melted, it grows brown feathers to blend in with rocks, soil and plants.

BRAVE LEMMINGS

In the winter, lemmings are hidden from some of their predators in their tunnels under the snow, although Arctic foxes seem to be able to find them easily and ermine, or stoats, are slim enough to chase lemmings through the tunnels. If lemmings are cornered, they put up a hostile defence. Their brightly patterned fur may serve to warn predators of their aggressive behaviour and unpleasant taste.

DANGEROUS NOSE

To warn off enemies or intimidate rivals, male hooded seals can inflate an extraordinary structure on their nose. This 'hood' is an enlargement of the nose cavity and can be inflated to form a vast sac about twice the size of a football. As well as the hood, male hooded seals can also force the lining of one nostril out through the other nostril to form a red balloon. When the seal shakes the balloon from side to side, it makes a loud 'pinging' noise.

HORN CIRCLE

Musk oxen are the size of ponies and are big and strong enough to have only two real predators – wolves and humans. Their horns are long, curved and sharply pointed with a solid horny band across the forehead. Males use their horns to fight for females but they are also useful for defence. A herd of musk oxen will form a tight circle, with their sharp horns facing outwards and calves or weaker animals sheltering in the middle. This strategy works well against wolves but is not very successful against people with guns.

COURTSHIP

At the start of the brief summer breeding season, many birds and mammals go through elaborate displays and ritual fights to make sure they find and keep the right partners for mating. Rival males, such as caribou, walruses and elephant seals fight each other for the right to mate with a group of females. Animals such as musk oxen and wolverines mark their territories with special smelly messages designed to keep out rival males or attract females. Pairs of Antarctic skuas use their long, loud calls for the same purpose. Courtship displays are usually loud and noisy affairs. They may take a great deal of effort and use up lots of energy.

At the same time, they make the courting animals very obvious to passing predators. But they are necessary to allow females to find the strongest and fittest males and to test whether the partners are ready and able to mate and care for young.

FENCING UNICORNS

The long tusk of the male narwhal, a type of Arctic whale, may have given rise to the legend of the unicorn. Tusks were sold in many countries long before people had seen the animal. Only male narwhals have a tusk and they may use them to fight other males. Males are sometimes seen 'fencing' with their tusks on the surface of the sea.

ELEPHANT SEALS

Male elephant seals are up to 10 times heavier than females and have a huge, swollen nose similar to an elephant's trunk. In the breeding season, the strongest males guard a group of females for mating. They fight rival males and roar challenges to them through their extraordinary nose, which acts like a loudspeaker. The oldest and biggest males usually win the fights. Males do not eat during the breeding season since they are constantly on guard on the breeding beaches. The beachmasters cannot afford to leave their females to catch food in the sea because another male will sneak in and take their place.

PENGUIN RITUALS

The striking golden-yellow neck and ear patches of the king penguin are used to attract a partner during courtship. Like other seabirds they need to display together to reinforce the pair bonds between partners before they can mate together.

CARIBOU

Male, or bull, caribou use their antlers during the autumn rut, or mating season. They have contests where they clash their antlers together or have neck-wrestling matches with their antlers locked together. These contests decide which of the bulls are strongest and best able to gather, and keep, a small group of cows safe from challenges by other bulls. After the rutting season, the bulls shed their antlers and grow new antlers for the next breeding season.

A pair of king penguins display their brightly coloured necks.

WANDERING ALBATROSSES

These magnificent birds live for over 80 years and tend to stick with one partner for life. When pairs are forming or newly formed, they take part in a long courtship display, but established pairs do not need much courtship. During the display, the male attracts a female by pointing his beak upwards, holding out his wings and whistling. When a female arrives, the two birds dance face to face. They make a variety of noises, clap their bills together loudly and fence with their huge, hooked bills. When they have paired up, the birds sit side by side on the nest area, nibbling each other's necks and calling softly.

Crested penguins swing their heads in a wide arc.

Adélie penguins bow during pair-bonding.

King penguins have a special 'advertising' call.

POLAR BEARS

Polar bear cubs stay with their mother for at least a year while she teaches them to hunt and survive in the Arctic. For the first few months she feeds the cubs on her rich milk, which is about 30 per cent fat. At birth, the cubs are helpless and tiny – only about a thousandth of their mother's weight. They are well protected from the weather and predators inside a warm snow den, dug by their mother. While she is in the den, the mother polar bear cannot feed and lives off fat stored in her body.

NESTS, EGGS & YOUNG

Most polar animals lay their eggs or give birth to their young in the brief summer. In fact, many animals only visit these regions for breeding. They choose to come to these hostile places because there is plenty of food in summer, as well as more space and fewer predators than in warmer places. Two exceptions to the summer breeding cycle are emperor penguins and polar bears, which both rear their young through the winter months. The richest food in polar regions is in the sea and many parents have to take it in turns to look after the young while their partner goes off to feed. Sometimes they may leave the young on their own or gathered in crèches.

FEATHER NEST

The female eider duck plucks soft down feathers from her own breast and uses them to line her nest. These fluffy feathers trap warm air and help to keep the eggs warm so they develop properly. If the parent birds have to leave the nest, they pull the down feathers over the nest like a warm duvet. Eider ducks nest on small, remote islands in the Arctic Ocean but their eggs and young are still in danger from predators; such as gulls and foxes, as well as the weather.

SNOWY OWLS

When there is plenty of food, such as mice, voles and lemmings, snowy owls may raise seven or eight chicks in one year. If food is scarce, they may not nest at all. The nest is a shallow scrape on the ground, lined with moss or feathers. Owls do not lay all their eggs at once, so there may be chicks of different sizes in the nest. If there is not enough food to go round, the largest owlet will eat the smallest and then the next smallest, and so on. This rather cruel behaviour ensures that at least one youngster has a chance of surviving.

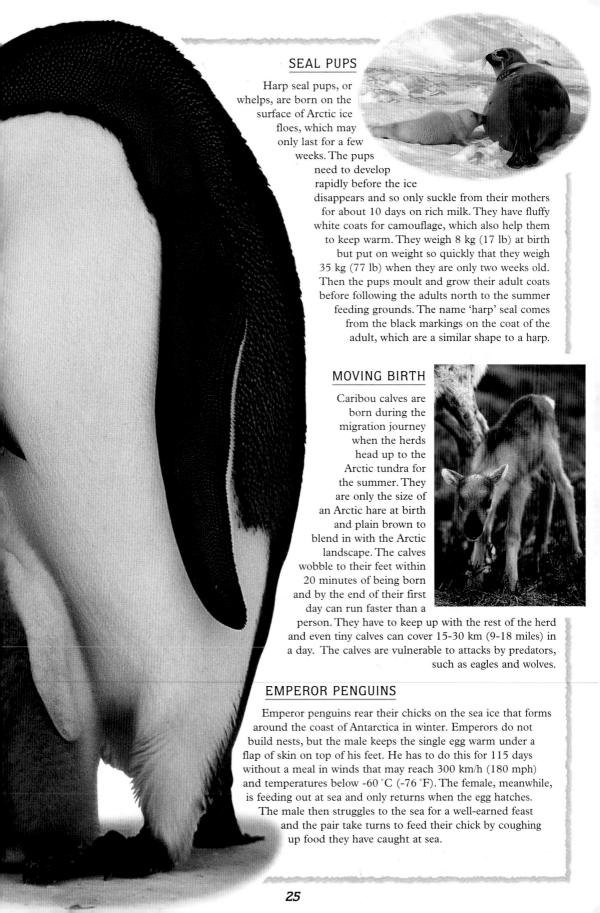

SEAL PUPS

Harp seal pups, or whelps, are born on the surface of Arctic ice floes, which may only last for a few weeks. The pups need to develop rapidly before the ice disappears and so only suckle from their mothers for about 10 days on rich milk. They have fluffy white coats for camouflage, which also help them to keep warm. They weigh 8 kg (17 lb) at birth but put on weight so quickly that they weigh 35 kg (77 lb) when they are only two weeks old. Then the pups moult and grow their adult coats before following the adults north to the summer feeding grounds. The name 'harp' seal comes from the black markings on the coat of the adult, which are a similar shape to a harp.

MOVING BIRTH

Caribou calves are born during the migration journey when the herds head up to the Arctic tundra for the summer. They are only the size of an Arctic hare at birth and plain brown to blend in with the Arctic landscape. The calves wobble to their feet within 20 minutes of being born and by the end of their first day can run faster than a person. They have to keep up with the rest of the herd and even tiny calves can cover 15-30 km (9-18 miles) in a day. The calves are vulnerable to attacks by predators, such as eagles and wolves.

EMPEROR PENGUINS

Emperor penguins rear their chicks on the sea ice that forms around the coast of Antarctica in winter. Emperors do not build nests, but the male keeps the single egg warm under a flap of skin on top of his feet. He has to do this for 115 days without a meal in winds that may reach 300 km/h (180 mph) and temperatures below -60 °C (-76 °F). The female, meanwhile, is feeding out at sea and only returns when the egg hatches. The male then struggles to the sea for a well-earned feast and the pair take turns to feed their chick by coughing up food they have caught at sea.

LIVING TOGETHER

Living in groups mainly for the breeding season is common in many polar animals such as sea birds, penguins and some seals. But other polar animals live in groups with an organized social structure all year round, sometimes with a leader that keeps them all together. In these groups, the young stay with their mothers or both parents for a year or more, learning how to survive. Usually only the female young stay in the group and the males leave to mate with females outside their own family. Relationships between the individuals in a group can become quite complex, with some animals becoming more important than others and each animal having its own place in the group. Group living has many advantages, from helping each other to find food and stopping other animals from stealing food, to banding together to fight predators and protect the young.

KILLER WHALES

Hunting in groups called pods, killer whales co-ordinate their movements by constantly making clicking and calling sounds to each other. The pod hunt like a pack of wolves on land. They attack narwhals, beluga whales and seals, sometimes tipping seals off ice floes. Group hunting allows killer whales to overcome very large prey, such as blue whales, the largest animals in the world.

CARIBOU

The largest herd of caribou in the world is probably the George River herd of North America, which is made up of 750,000 animals, but smaller herds may be thousands strong. For most of the year, herds of caribou are made up of females and their young. Mature males usually live separately from the females and sometimes move together in compact bands of between 100 and 1,000 animals. The only time when males and females of all ages come together is during the autumn breeding, or rutting, season. Then the adult males fight to keep a group of between five and forty females for mating. The females move freely between groups held by different males, leaving and joining them when they want to.

WOLVES

The body language of the wolves within a pack shows their status or ranking within the group. A top, or dominant, wolf will stand erect with its ears and tail pointing upwards. It may also show its teeth and growl. A subordinate, or low-ranking, wolf (on the left of the picture) crouches down, turns down its ears and holds its tail between its legs. Instead of growling, it whines to show it recognizes that the other wolf is superior. Every time one wolf meets another, they use their body language to confirm their status in the group. Only the top male and the top female in a wolf pack have cubs. The ranking system within a pack helps the group to survive as they co-operate to catch food and rear young in a hostile environment.

MUSK OXEN

A herd of musk oxen is made up of females and their young, led by one or more strong males, or bulls. In the mating season, younger bulls are driven out of the herd and form all-male bachelor herds, or live on their own. When they grow stronger, they may challenge the master bulls for control of their own herd. In summer, musk oxen live in herds of about 10 animals, but in winter, the herds join up to form groups of 50 or more.

PEOPLE AT THE POLES

ICE SHELTERS

The Inuit igloo, made of a dome of snow blocks, was a temporary shelter, used on hunting trips. Some Inuit still build igloos for this reason today. The inner walls of an igloo are covered in snow, which melts and freezes into a smooth covering of ice. This igloo is lit by a modern pressure lamp, but light and heat were originally provided by oil lamps burning animal blubber. With the addition of body heat, the igloos keep surprisingly warm inside. In winter, the Inuit traditionally lived in houses made of stone and turf and in summer, they moved into skin tents.

For thousands of years, people, such as the Inuit of North America and Greenland, the Sami of Scandinavia and Russia, and the Nenets of Siberia, have lived in the Arctic. Their bodies have become adapted to tolerate the cold and they have developed nomadic, or travelling lifestyles based on hunting wild animals, such as caribou, seals and fish. European explorers, intent on reaching the poles, learned much from the traditional survival skills of these peoples whose tools, clothing and transport were perfectly designed for the harsh polar conditions. Today, the Inuit and other Arctic peoples are abandoning their traditional lifestyles. Most have settled in modern homes, go to the shops for their food and work on modern fishing boats or in mines. In the summer, however, some still go out hunting and fishing, and combine the old and new ways of life.

POLAR TRANSPORT

Modern forms of Arctic transport, such as this motorized toboggan or skidoo, have replaced the traditional dog sledges. They are easier to keep than a team of dogs and their owners can buy fuel and oil instead of having to catch seals to feed to their dogs.

INUIT PEOPLES

Inuit people have many physical features to help them survive in the cold of Arctic lands. They are short and solidly built to help their bodies conserve heat. The thick pads of fat on their cheeks and eyelids help to protect those parts of the body which are exposed to the cold. The heavy eyelids also protect the eyes from the glare of the Sun reflecting off the white snow. Traditional clothing was based on the skins and fur of animals such as caribou, seals and polar bears. This mother is carrying her baby son in a sealskin amaut.

PEOPLE IN THE ANTARCTIC

There are no native inhabitants of the Antarctic and it was only about 200 years ago that explorers first set foot on the Antarctic continent. Today, many people make scientific expeditions to the Antarctic to study the weather, the wildlife, the ice and the rocks. Most of them go there just for a few months in summer, though some stay for the winter. This huge dome protects the buildings of the United States' Amundsen-Scott base at the South Pole.

REINDEER PEOPLE

This Nenet woman, from Siberia, is using her domesticated reindeer to pull a sledge full of her belongings. The reindeer have colourful red and yellow blankets and harnesses. Like the Sami people, the Nenets follow the reindeer herds, eating reindeer meat, milk and cheese and using reindeer skins for making clothes and for trading in other goods. Today, most have settled in permanent villages.

MODERN PEOPLE

Arctic people have endured some of the most difficult living conditions on Earth by making use of animals and materials in their frozen environment. But modern technology has now transformed their lives, allowing them to live more comfortably in a world of centrally-heated homes, motorized transport, synthetic clothing, high-tech weapons, shops and computers. Traditional survival skills are no longer so relevant.

SAMI PEOPLE

The Sami, or Lapp, people of Scandinavia and Russia hunted reindeer from earliest times and used to survive by keeping large herds. They followed the reindeer on their migration, stopping whenever the herd stopped to feed and sometimes helping them across rivers. Some Sami still live in this way today, although the herders' families usually stay in permanent settlements.

PROTECTING THE POLES

The polar regions are important to the survival of the whole Earth. If the polar ice caps melted, less of the Sun's rays would be reflected back into space and the Earth's climate would heat up. If the world's oceans get warmer, they will expand and this, together with all the melted ice, would raise sea levels. Also, the polar plants and animals are part of a big interconnected web of life that maintains life as we know it. If polar wildlife is damaged, it affects other areas too. Environmental problems in polar regions include pollution, damage from mining and drilling, and hunting endangered species. Today, scientific research has shown how fragile the polar lands are and laws have been passed to try to minimize damage and protect these unique and extraordinary regions for the future.

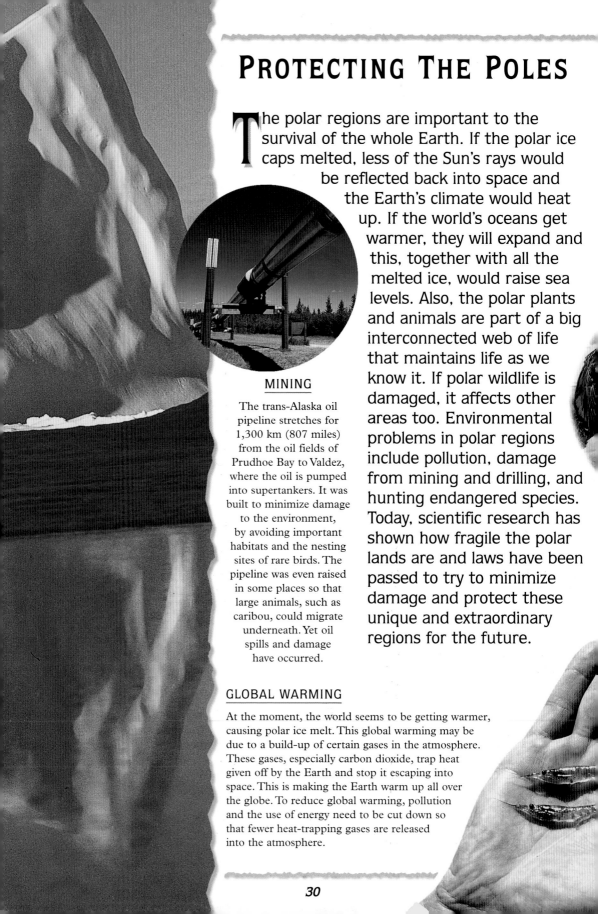

MINING

The trans-Alaska oil pipeline stretches for 1,300 km (807 miles) from the oil fields of Prudhoe Bay to Valdez, where the oil is pumped into supertankers. It was built to minimize damage to the environment, by avoiding important habitats and the nesting sites of rare birds. The pipeline was even raised in some places so that large animals, such as caribou, could migrate underneath. Yet oil spills and damage have occurred.

GLOBAL WARMING

At the moment, the world seems to be getting warmer, causing polar ice melt. This global warming may be due to a build-up of certain gases in the atmosphere. These gases, especially carbon dioxide, trap heat given off by the Earth and stop it escaping into space. This is making the Earth warm up all over the globe. To reduce global warming, pollution and the use of energy need to be cut down so that fewer heat-trapping gases are released into the atmosphere.

HARD TO REACH

The severe weather and difficult terrain of polar regions has helped to protect them from exploitation over the years. But today, with advanced methods of transport and technology, icebreaker ships can even smash their way through to the North Pole. The abundant wildlife and rich mineral resources, such as coal and oil act like a magnet, drawing people towards the poles. Polar resources will become ever more important as those in other parts of the world are depleted.

NORTH
POLE

NEW YORK
5,461 Km

LONDON
4,292 Km

ROME
5,439 Km

MOSCOW
4,348 Km

SOUTH POLE
20,000 Km

TOURISM

In the Arctic, tourism is well established and there are wildlife tours and hiking trips. Even in the Antarctic, tourist ships allow their passengers to get really close to sea birds, seals and whales, some of which are very tame (see left). By visiting these beautiful places, people understand the need to protect them. Tourists also bring income and employment to the local people, but they can disturb the habitats and the wildlife they come to see. Their numbers and movements need to be controlled for the sake of the environment.

SCIENTIFIC RESEARCH

Launching weather balloons in the Antarctic is just one of many experiments carried out by scientists to help them understand how the polar regions work. Holes in the ozone layer were first discovered over the Antarctic, and are probably caused by gases called CFCs, which come from such products as refrigerators and aerosols. Ozone holes are larger over the poles because of their special weather conditions. The ozone layer is vital to the planet because it stops most of the Sun's ultraviolet rays from reaching the Earth. Large doses of these rays damage living things.

FUTURE FOOD

Krill are tiny, shrimp-like animals less than 5 cm (2 inches) long, yet they are the most important Antarctic animals. They are food for millions of fish, birds, seals and whales. Since whaling bans were introduced to protect endangered species, fishermen have started to catch krill instead. Krill are almost half protein and are rich in vitamins. The harvesting of krill needs to be carefully monitored to see how it affects other Antarctic animals who depend on the krill for their survival, just as annual meetings are held to decide how much fish and squid can be caught in the Southern Ocean.

FIND OUT MORE

Useful Addresses

To find out more about polar regions, or the protection of polar wildlife, here are some organizations who may be able to help.

THE SCOTT POLAR RESEARCH INSTITUTE,
Lensfield Road, Cambridge CB2 1ER
(01223 3365440)

WWF-UK,
Panda House, Weyside Park, Goldalming, Surrey GU7 1XR
(01483 426444)

GREENPEACE UK,
Canonbury Villas, London N1 2PN
(0171 865 8100)

THE EDUCATION DEPARTMENT AT LONDON ZOO,
Regents Park, London NW1 4RY.
To adopt an animal write to Lifewatch at the same address.

ROYAL SOCIETY FOR THE PROTECTION OF BIRDS,
The Lodge, Sandy, Bedfordshire, SG19 2DL (01767 680551)

BRITISH ANTARCTIC SURVEY,
Natural Environment Research Council, High Cross, Madingley Road, Cambridge CB3 0ET
(01223 221400)

THE PITT RIVERS MUSEUM,
Parks Road, Oxford. Exhibits include peoples of the Arctic.
(Information line: 01865 270949)

Useful websites

THE ARCTIC STUDIES CENTER
http://nmnhwww.si.edu/arctic

ARCTIC & ANTARCTIC INFORMATION SITE
http://www.arcticsurvey.com

ACKNOWLEDGEMENTS

We would like to thank: Graham Rich, Rosalind Beckman and Elizabeth Wiggans for their ass
Copyright © 2003 ticktock Entertainment Ltd.
First published in Great Britain by ticktock Publishing Ltd., Unit 2, Orchard Business Centr
Kent TN2 3XF, Great Britain.
All rights reserved.
No part of this publication may be reproduced, stored in a retrieval system, or transmitted in any
photocopying, recording or otherwise, without prior written permission o
A CIP catalogue record for this book is available from the British Library

Picture research by Image Select. Printed in China.

Picture Credits: t=top, b=bottom, c=centre, l=left, r=right, OFC=outside front cover, OBC

AKG Photo; 3rb. B&C Alexander Photography; 2l, 2c, 2/3t, 3tl, 4tl, 4/5 (main pic), 5c, 6tl, ?
12/13b + 32, 12/13c, 14/15 (main pic), 15tr, 15cr, 16l, 18br, 18cl, 18tc, 18/19t, 22tl, 22/23b, 2
25/26c, 26tr, 28bc, 28bl, 28tl, 29bl, 29br, 29c, 29tl, 30l, 30/31bc, 31cl, 31tr. Oxford Scientific F
16c, 18cr, 19tc, 20tl, 21br, 21tr, 21tl, 21rc, 24bl, 24/25c, 25tr, 31br. Planet Earth Pictures; IFC
16/17b, 17cl, 17tl, 17tr, 19b, 20/21c, 20/21b, 23tl, 30cl. Survi

Every effort has been made to trace the copyright holders and we apologize in adva
We would be pleased to insert the appropriate acknowledgement in any subseq